What Veterinarians Need to Know

Joe Rhatigan

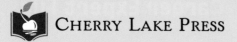
CHERRY LAKE PRESS

Published in the United States of America by Cherry Lake Publishing Group
Ann Arbor, Michigan
www.cherrylakepublishing.com

Reading Adviser: Beth Walker Gambro, MS, Ed., Reading Consultant, Yorkville, IL

Photo Credits: © hedgehog94/Shutterstock, cover, 1; © hedgehog94/Shutterstock, 5; © 135pixels/Shutterstock, 7; © KOTOIMAGES/Shutterstock, 8; © Rembolle/Shutterstock, 9; © Gemma Campling/Shutterstock, 10; © PeopleImages.com – Yuri A/Shutterstock, 11; © 4 PM production/Shutterstock, 13; © SeventyFour/Shutterstock, 14; © Ermolaev Alexander/Shutterstock, 15; © RJ22/Shutterstock, 16; © Hryshchyshen Serhii/Shutterstock, 17; © AnnaStills/Shutterstock, 19; © Prostock-studio/Shutterstock, 20; © Deni Williams/Shutterstock,21; © SeventyFour/Shutterstock, 23; © Blachkovsky/Shutterstock, 24; © Pressmaster/Shutterstock, 27; © Try_my_best/Shutterstock, 28; © Alberto Menendez Cervero/Shutterstock, 29

Cherry Lake Press is an imprint of Cherry Lake Publishing Group.

Library of Congress Cataloging-in-Publication Data

Names: Rhatigan, Joe, author.
Title: What veterinarians need to know / written by: Joe Rhatigan.
Description: Ann Arbor, Michigan : Cherry Lake Publishing, [2024] | Series: Career expert files | Audience: Grades 4-6 | Summary: "Veterinarians need to have the expert knowledge, skills, and tools to keep the world's animals healthy. The Career Expert Files series covers professionals who are experts in their fields. These career experts know things we never thought they'd need to know, but we're glad they do"— Provided by publisher.
Identifiers: LCCN 2023035044 | ISBN 9781668939178 (paperback) | ISBN 9781668938133 (hardcover) | ISBN 9781668940518 (ebook) | ISBN 9781668941867 (pdf)
Subjects: LCSH: Veterinarians—Juvenile literature. | Veterinary medicine—Vocational guidance—Juvenile literature.
Classification: LCC SF756 .R43 2024 | DDC 636.089—dc23/eng/20230818
LC record available at https://lccn.loc.gov/2023035044

Cherry Lake Publishing Group would like to acknowledge the work of the Partnership for 21st Century Learning, a Network of Battelle for Kids. Please visit Battelle for Kids online for more information.

Printed in the United States of America

Note from publisher: Websites change regularly, and their future contents are outside of our control. Supervise children when conducting any recommended online searches for extended learning opportunities.

Joe Rhatigan lives in Western North Carolina with his family and Jumbo Shrimp, a cat, and Rooster, a dog. He writes, edits, reads, buys, and adores books.

CONTENTS

In the Know

Every career you can imagine has one thing in common. It takes an expert. Career experts need to know more about how to do a specific job than other people do. That's how everyone from plumbers to rocket scientists get their job done.

Sometimes it takes years of college study to learn what they need to know. Other times, people learn by working alongside someone who is already a career expert. No matter how they learn, it takes a career expert to do any job well.

Take veterinarians, for instance. These professionals know how to treat and care for pets, farm animals, zoo animals, and even animals in the wild. They know about diseases, nutrition, healing injuries, animal anatomy, and so much more.

Does the idea of working with animals appeal to you? Would you like to build a career as a veterinarian? Here are some things you need to know.

Veterinarians are Good at:

- Interacting with animals

- Communicating with people about complex topics

- Problem-solving

CHAPTER 1

Veterinarians Know... How to Keep Animals Healthy

You go to the pediatrician for your annual health checkup. You go to the dentist to get your teeth cleaned. For your eyes, you go to an optometrist. You might even need a surgeon. That's a lot of doctors! Animals need all those types of doctors, too. But they go to the same one. An animal doctor is a veterinarian, also called a vet.

Vets use their knowledge and skills to keep animals healthy. Vets **diagnose** and treat all sorts of animals. They teach humans how to properly care for their pets. They teach them how to care for their domestic animals.

Vets work in different places. More than half work in clinics with household pets. Others work in animal hospitals. Some make house calls to farms. There are many kinds of vets.

Cows can grow to weigh nearly 1,500 pounds (680.4 kilograms)!
That's about 150 times the size of an average household cat.

Some people enjoy keeping exotic animals as pets, like lizards, snakes, and even tarantulas!

They all have one thing in common. They all have a lot of compassion for animals. They love animals—just like you do!

The vet you're probably most familiar with is your pet's. This vet works in a clinic. There, vets and their staff care for our animals. This includes dogs, cats, reptiles, birds, hamsters, ferrets, and fish. These vets make sure your animals have the right food. But not too much of it! They check for diseases. They treat injuries. If surgery is needed, many vets do the operation, too.

VETERINARIAN'S OATH

An oath is a promise. All brand-new veterinarians must take the same oath. The Veterinarian's Oath is only 87 words. But it packs in a lot of promises. First, they promise to use their knowledge to help animals. They promise to help animals stay healthy and happy. Next, they agree to prevent and relieve animal suffering. They also pledge to protect natural animal habitats. They promise to help prevent diseases and improve medical knowledge. That's a lot of promises! And vets do their best to keep them all. What oath do you think pet owners should make? Write down your promises on a separate sheet of paper.

Just like humans, giraffes have only seven vertebrae, but unlike us, their necks can reach up to 6 feet (1.8 meters) in length!

Just like you take your dog or cat to the vet, farm animals need periodic checkups from veterinarians for their health, too!

Zoo animals need vets, too! These vets must know all about elephants, tigers, and more. They need to know how much each animal eats. They need to know whether or not they need shots. They need to know how to make their habitats comfortable. They try to make their habitats as natural as they can. These vets may also work with wildlife or aquatic species.

Vets also care for cows, pigs, sheep, goats, and horses. Vets who attend to farmers' animals often make house calls. At the farm, vets do things a pet vet does. They may help animals give birth. Farmers depend on vets to keep their animals healthy.

CHAPTER 2

Veterinarians Know... How to Make a Living Caring for Animals

You bring your dog, Cookie, to the vet. It's something you do every year. The vet has Cookie's chart. The chart has information from all of Cookie's earlier visits. The chart will tell the vet Cookie's history. It will tell her if he needs vaccinations. It will tell her if he's due for tests. It will help her keep track of Cookie's care.

The vet examines Cookie's eyes, ears, and nose. She listens to his heart and lungs. She opens his mouth and looks at his teeth. She takes samples to study. She may ask you a few questions. This is called a checkup. It's just one of the ways vets interact with animals. This helps them do their jobs well.

Pets may have some anxiety when going to the vet. Try to make them as comfortable as possible.

From cats to zebras, vets don't just examine the animal. They also talk to the animal's caregiver. Vets give clients important information to care for their animals. They provide information on nutrition, exercise, grooming, and housing. Vets know that animal owners must do their part. Together with vets, caregivers keep their animals safe and healthy. They can spot problems before they get too serious.

When you don't feel well, you tell a parent. If you get hurt, you say "ouch." Animals don't talk, but they do communicate in other ways. Vets know how to "listen" to animals. Then they can tell if an animal is in pain. They may ask the animal's owner some questions. *Is your pet more tired than usual? Is he eating or drinking less? Or more?* A vet may draw blood to test for **infections**. He may test a **stool** sample for **parasites**. Parasites include tapeworms, roundworms, and hookworms. This all helps the vet discover what is wrong.

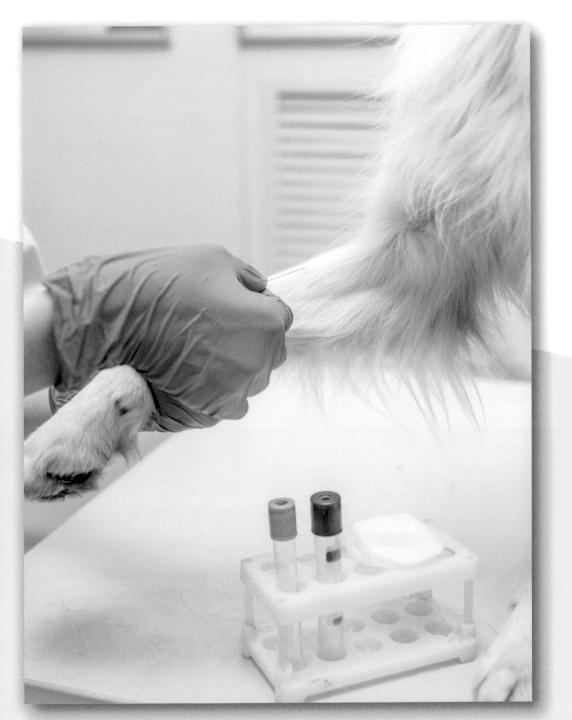

If a veterinarian draws blood from your pet, they will send it off to a laboratory for testing. These tests can help them determine if your pet is healthy.

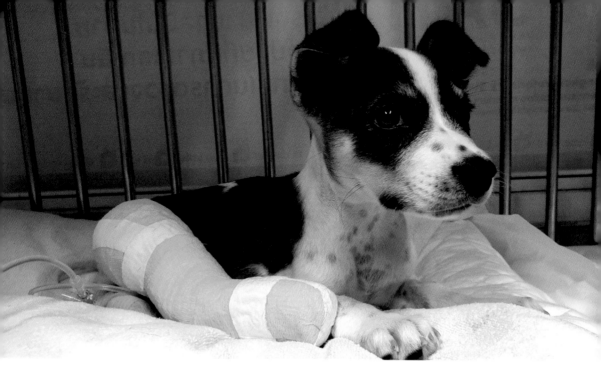

Dogs are very active creatures and can fracture or break bones, just like us! For adult dogs, it can take up to 8 weeks for their bones to sufficiently heal and return to normal.

Animals with wounds may get stitches. Animals with a broken leg need a cast. Animals need medication to get rid of a parasite. Once vets identify the problem, they quickly get to work! They know the right medicines and dosages to give. They also know when surgery is needed.

Farms usually want some of their animals to have offspring. Zoos do, too! Vets can help with that by giving advice. They can help provide an environment free from stress. This is very important when it comes to endangered species.

People with pets, however, usually want the opposite. They want to make sure their pets don't reproduce. That is because there is an overpopulation of many pets. Vets perform simple surgeries called **spays** for females. There are surgeries called **neuters** for males. These surgeries make it so animals cannot reproduce.

A SOLEMN RESPONSIBILITY

Sometimes animals cannot get well. These animals need special help. A vet will have to help the animal's owner decide. Do we let the animal live in pain? Or do we perform **euthanasia**? Euthanasia means ending an animal's life in a kind way. Vets never take this decision lightly. It is a last resort. They consider it a privilege to help struggling animals die. They want to help them die peacefully and without pain.

CHAPTER 3

Veterinarians Know... The Tools of the Trade

Vets are doctors. They use many of the tools that our doctors use!

Tools used for checkups include a stethoscope. Vets use it to listen to an animal's heart and lungs. Vets also use thermometers to check for fever. An otoscope is a magnifying lens with a light. It is used to examine ears for infections or parasites. For eyes, vets use an ophthalmoscope. This lets vets look at the back of the eye. They can see the health of the retina and nerves.

Both veterinarians and doctors use stethoscopes to listen to the rhythms in the hearts of their patients.

X-rays can be potentially harmful to animals. Radiologists wear special protective gowns and place protective cover on the parts of the animal that are not being x-rayed.

Vets use x-ray machines to take images of bones. They are looking for breaks or fractures. An **ultrasound** machine uses sounds to take pictures of organs. Ultrasounds can find tumors and blockages. A vet or a technician sometimes uses a microscope. They can examine blood, skin, and stool samples. Vets are looking for parasites. They're looking for microorganisms. They're looking for dangerous cells that can lead to cancer.

Vets use scalpels, forceps, scissors, and needle holders. They use these tools for surgeries and wound repair. They have anesthesia machines to help animals sleep. Animals sleep during surgeries and dental cleanings.

LIFE AT A WILDLIFE CLINIC

Some vets train to take care of wild animals. They deal with animals with injuries. They also test animals for diseases. These diseases can make other animals or people sick. Hurt animals are often brought to a wildlife clinic. Once these animals heal, they're safely returned to their habitat. Vets also **sedate** animals in the wild. Then they can work on them right there! Why? Because it can be difficult taking an elephant in for its checkup! Ask an adult to help you find TV shows about wildlife vets. There are a lot of options!

CHAPTER 4

Veterinarians Know... How to Work with Animals Safely

Vets have to practice safety, just like medical doctors. For vets, however, they have something else to worry about. They have to keep themselves safe with their patients!

Dogs bite. Cats scratch. They usually do these things when they are scared. Sometimes they do these things when stressed. Vets learn how to create a calm environment for animals. Vets also know how to safely restrain animals. They do all they can to avoid bites and scratches. If an injury occurs, vets know how to clean wounds.

Vets use needles, scissors, and even scalpels. They know how to handle sharp medical devices, or sharps.

Vet techs work hard to help keep animals calm. They may pet the animal, hold the animal still, or reward the animal with treats.

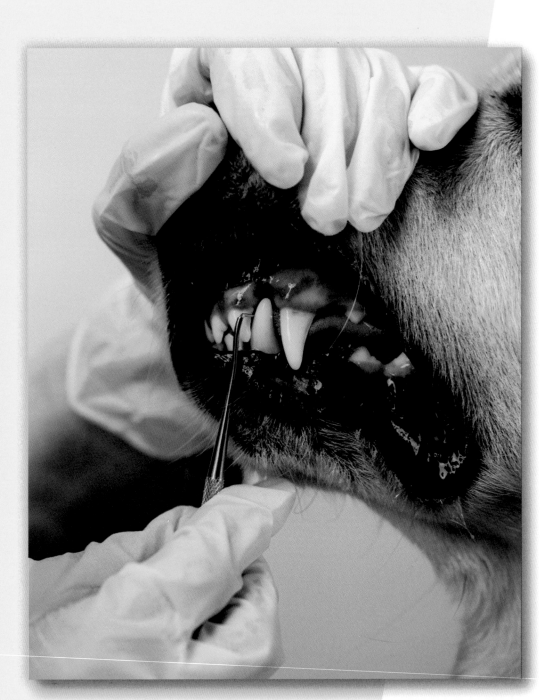

Dogs have sharp teeth on both sides of their mouth called canines, meant specifically for puncturing their food or holding onto toys and bones.

Dogs and cats pee or vomit sometimes. This can cause a slipping hazard. Vets train their staff to clean up accidents immediately. Vets also practice safe lifting practices. They use these when picking up large animals. This way, they don't hurt themselves.

Large animals such as horses and cattle can be dangerous. Vets watch out for an animal charging or kicking. Vets also must be careful with sedated wild animals. They need to stay away from claws and jaws if an animal wakes up unexpectedly.

CREATING A STRESS-FREE ENVIRONMENT

Going to the doctor can be stressful—especially for pets. Veterinarians and their staff know what to do to help. For example, some vets create different entrances for dogs and cats. Some have different dog and cat waiting areas. Often, tasty treats are at the front desk. They're often near the weighing scale. They're often in the exam rooms. Vet clinics try to avoid loud noises. They try to avoid separating pets from their owners. Vets know how to read animal body language. If an animal is stressed, the vet will know how to approach it. They will know how to approach without causing more anxiety.

CHAPTER 5

Veterinarians Know... How to Find the Job They Want

More than 87 million homes in the United States have a pet. That's a lot of dogs, cats, fish, hamsters, and birds. All those pets need vets!

First, you have to graduate from a 4-year college. During that time, you should study biology. You should study **zoology**. You should study other sciences. You also need to get some hands-on experience with animals. Then you need to get into a vet program at a university. This program will be at least 4 more years. Then you receive your Doctor of Veterinary Medicine degree. After this, you have to pass a state test. Then you can start practicing.

If you are passionate about caring for animals, you might want to think about becoming a veterinarian! It might just be the perfect career for you.

Many vets work in hospitals or clinics. Others start their own practices. Still, others go to school for even longer. Then they can specialize in different areas. These areas include eye care, dentistry, or animal behavior. A vet could also specialize in internal medicine.

WHAT'S A VET TECH?

A veterinarian technician works closely with the veterinarian. They help prepare animals, equipment, medicines, and more. They are like nurses for animals! They collect samples. They perform certain procedures and help during surgery. Oftentimes, vet techs will greet the pets. They'll lead them to the exam room. You need a 2-year college degree to be a vet tech. It's a great job for animal lovers! Especially those who don't want to or can't go through 8 years of school!

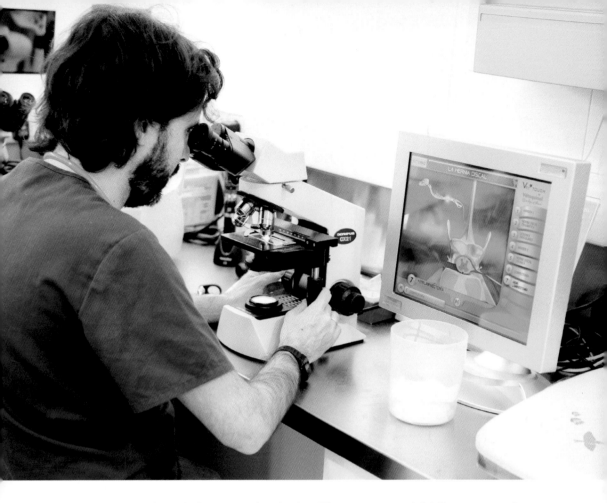

It takes many people to help a veterinarian's office run smoothly! From vet techs to laboratory technicians, each person has an important role to play to make sure your pet is getting the best care.

Not all vets treat animals. Some become teachers. Others conduct research on animal behavior or diseases. Veterinarians can travel the world to work with endangered species. They can work with search and rescue dogs. Vets have even been sent into space!

Activity

Stop, Think, and Write

Can you imagine a world without veterinarians? What would we do if a pet got sick? Get a separate sheet of paper. On one side, answer these questions:

- *How do veterinarians make the world a better place?*
- *If you were a veterinarian, what types of animals would you like to care for?*
- *Where would you like to work?*

On the other side of the paper:

- *Draw a picture of you as a veterinarian in your vet's office!*

Things to Do If You Want to Be a Veterinarian

Many people get the experience they need to become a veterinarian because they know from a young age that this is exactly what they want to be when they grow up!

NOW

- Volunteer at an animal shelter. Animal shelters are places where you can get hands-on experience with animals. They often need help cleaning, feeding, and exercising the animals.

- Offer to walk neighbors' dogs or pet-sit.

- Look for opportunities to volunteer at a farm or a zoo.

- If you can, foster or adopt a dog, cat, or other animal.

LATER

- Check out summer programs for high school students to experience vets in action.

- Get a job at a vet clinic as an assistant or receptionist.

- Once you're in college, focus on biology, chemistry, biochemistry, and zoology classes. Make sure you have lots of hands-on experience with animals as well—vet programs insist on it!

Learn More

Books

Bedell, J. M. *So, You Want to Work with Animals?*. New York, NY: Aladdin/Beyond Words, 2017.

Martin, Steve. *Vet Academy: Are You Ready for the Challenge?* San Diego, CA: Kane Miller Books, 2014.

Reeves, Diane Lindsey. *Do You Like Taking Care of Animals?* Ann Arbor, MI: Cherry Lake, 2023.

Wild, Gabby, and Jennifer Symanski. *Wild Vet Adventures: Saving Animals Around the World with Dr. Gabby Wild.* Washington, DC: National Geographic Kids, 2021.

On the Web

With an adult, learn more online with these suggested searches.

The Center for Veterinary Medicine's kid page

A Veterinary Medicine Activity Book for kids from Purdue University

Vet Set Go

Glossary

diagnose (DIYE-ig-nohs) examine a patient's symptoms to figure out what is causing an illness

euthanasia (yoo-thuh-NAY-juh) a painless procedure to end an animal's life to stop it from suffering

infections (in-FEK-shuhnz) when germs get into a body and multiply, making the person or animal sick

neuters (NOO-tuhrz) surgeries to remove the reproductive organs from male animals

parasites (PER-uh-siyts) organisms that live inside another living thing

sedate (sih-DAYT) to use a medicine to make a patient feel calm or sleepy

spays (SPAYZ) surgeries to remove the reproductive organs from female animals

stool (STOOL) poop

ultrasound (UHL-truh-sownd) a machine that uses sounds to take pictures of internal body organs

zoology (zoh-AH-luh-jee) the study of animals

Index